T0358989

RETURN HOME

WORDS OF CLEARWATER

Arcadia Press Pty Ltd

Return Home – Words of Clearwater

Copyright © Daniel Littlewood.

Words of Clearwater – The Voice of Life, 1st print 2012
Words of Clearwater - Book 1, Truth. 1st print 1990
Words of Clearwater - Book 2, Love Yourself. 1st print 1992
Words of Clearwater - Book 3, Start to Live. 1st print 1992
Words of Clearwater - Book 4, Take My Hand. 1st print 1999

ISBN 978-0-9871625-6-4

Printed in Hong Kong

For more information: wordsofclearwater.com

Published by Arcadia Press Pty Ltd

arcadiapress.com.au

Country of publication: Australia

RETURN HOME

WORDS OF CLEARWATER

CONTENTS

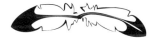

The words you read in this book were spoken by Clearwater, my brother of another lifetime.

He reaches out of the nothingness of the past to remind us that all life was given to us as a gift, that nothing is preordained, that each of us creates our future in every moment.

He asks us to gaze upon ourselves and know the wondrous creation that we are.

This book is a written transcript of an oral teaching given by Clearwater through Daniel Littlewood. For clarity, we have added words to the original information. This is in no way intended to change the meaning of the messages. All added words are in brackets.

MANY MOONS HAVE PASSED SINCE LAST WE SAT TOGETHER

There are many words to speak for such as I that come from the Grandfathers to walk amongst you, to give direction, to give hope, to give confirmation of thought.

This [is a] time of darkness and confusion when the warriors and the wise ones are brought together [so] that their energies might reach out into the universe. From the four directions they will come and around their shoulders will be the blanket of many colours. [It is] the time of the great gathering. Many teepees will come. The great council will be attended by many. For never before in the history of man have changes of such proportion been manifested. Never before have the energies of the universe been so powerful. Never before have the intelligences of other dimensions walked amongst you. The beings of Light, the silver ones of the stars, the vibrations of the creatures of the oceans, all reach out. [This is] the time of the tribes, the people of the earth, the children of our Mother. They have returned.

They have returned in such as you – those of you that have The Great Knowing, the remembrances of the time before memory when man truly walked in paradise, before the time of darkness when man lost control of his passions and saw himself as greater than that which had created him. Hear me my children, you are part of this gathering. You must be made aware of the power of your thoughts and of your words. You must come to understand that every action that you take reaches far out and affects the lives of all. For truly this is the evolution of man and of the universe.

In her sickness our Mother has called. [She has] called to her children that suckled from her breasts long ago and that passed into the shadows at the coming of darkness. For it was then that we drew our blankets around us and stepped back into the shadows. But hear me children – the time of existence is passing and the time of living will begin once more. I come to speak to those that have the ears to hear. I come with my brother that he will take my voice, for more will hear my voice than there are blades of grass upon the Great Plains. This I have said many times and it will be so.

But those that walk the path of my brother must walk with downcast eyes and speak in whispers. Not for you the mountain where you speak in a loud voice and call attention to yourselves... This is not for you. Only quietly as the summer breeze rustles the leaves, so will be your voices. For it is not by words that you will show others, it is how you live your lives. For when you find the well of spirituality, you shine like a bright star in the night sky and others gaze upon your beauty and your tranquility and they come to you seeking the calmness that you have found. And your voice will be added to my voice and those like me, for we are many in number and we call to you as you call to us.

We have need of you as you have need of us. For we do not impose ourselves upon you. We come to you in love.

All around you there is confusion and fear as old ideologies are swept away and old institutions crumble and our Mother begins to shake herself to rid herself of that which ails her. And you my children, each one of you has a part to play. But I do not come to speak words of fear. I come to speak to the warriors, for it takes the bravery of the warrior to stand tall in the time of darkness. For a true warrior is compassionate and humble. For his strength has been tried many times. His courage has been tested, as you, in each of your lifetimes have set trials for yourselves that you might vanquish your fears, that you might seek out your strengths and your weaknesses, that you might recognise yourself for what you are – a creation of the Great Spirit. That you have the ability to create with your thoughts and your words. Hear me my children, I have great love for you and great compassion.

There are those that have left the earth plane to walk in spirit that they might come to those that they love and become one with them, as my brother's woman walks in spirit. She walks amongst the stars and guides the souls of the children to the wombs of the mother. [This is] the time of the gentle ones to walk in spirit. Yet you fear death, yet it is nothing. It is part of life. Do not be afraid my children for you are loved as you are part of the Great Spirit. You are eternal. For you were never born and can never die. You are the wind, you are the rain, you are the sun. You are the coldness of winter, and the heat of summer. You are the hawk and the eagle. The mountain and the forest. You are the very earth itself. You are our Mother. And you are beauty, but you have forgotten. In your sleep you have forgotten. In the logicality of your thoughts you have forgotten. But now, such as you that were chosen to walk the path of the seeker, chosen by the Grandfathers, the strongest of the strong, the bravest of the brave to walk before the people, now is your time and I come to remind you. [I come] so that the ember of memory that lives in your heart will be fanned into a flame, so that you will remember the time of the oneness when the Sun People walked the lands who were one with all things. They sought domain over none. [It was] the time of harmony when you could leave your bodies and journey amongst the stars to learn at the feet of other dimensions. For you are many things my children. Look inside yourself. See the beauty that you are.

The ones from the womb now are the first of the Spiritual Ones. It is for these that you have returned to find them places of sanctuary where they may be protected. Where they may grow and flourish. For it is their children that will walk in paradise. The One-Tribe, the One-People. Brother will not prey upon brother. Sister will embrace sister. The time of the Sun People will return.

I have much that I will share with you. And I wish you to know of me. But I do not come as a teacher. I come as a friend. For long have I walked the lands and much have I seen. But I have no existence without you. And our task cannot be completed without your vibrations.

Children hear me.

The time of darkness will pass. Do

not be afraid. There will be great pain and much fear. Each one chose this task. You will be ridiculed and the time will come when those that walk this path [are] persecuted. For the ones that control and manipulate walk in fear. They fear that their power will be taken from them, that you will regain your freedom, and it will be so. But the battle gains momentum. And so the warriors come. Our Mother brings them together and I carry the message. You carry the sacred bundle of the people, be conscious of this. For I will speak only to those that have the ears to hear and I will show those that have the eyes to see. But I will stand aside from those that speak in a loud voice and those that seek personal satisfaction. Only the quiet ones will I come to.

I and those like me are many in number. As man steps out of his logical thought and once again becomes free then you will be our bridge. Man and Spirit once more hand in hand. Loved ones of long ago will come together. The bond of the heart is binding – it cannot be severed. You will recognise brother and sister, lover, husband, son and daughter. But the recognition will come from the heart. Truly the tribes are gathering and the smoke from their fires will fill the sky. And the sage and the sweet grass will envelope all.

I will come to you many times as my brother walks this land. But as we walk we prepare for another journey.

Children, gaze above you, Grandfather Eagle flies. He is your protection. The spirit of fire and of water, of the earth and of the sky comes to you to give you warmth and sustenance, to give you strength and protection.

Long has my brother travelled the path of the seeker. Our people yearn for his return. But there is much yet to be accomplished. Be proud my children. Look into your hearts. Walk in joy and happiness that you have come together again, one to support the other. You will remember. These are my words and this is my gift. I give you my heart, let it beat with yours. Come from your hearts my children. For you are children of the universe. The earth is your Mother. Love her as she loves you. Send out your thoughts of healing. Let it embrace her. For she has great need of you.

We are the people. We are the tribes. We are the human beings. Hear me, for the Great Council comes together and I, Clearwater, brother of Sun-In-Face will speak. Take my energy and my strength. Take my knowledge and my wisdom. When you gaze at me you gaze at self. For there is none wiser than you. Remember, you are perfection. Walk in peace my children. There are many such as I that will come and share their wisdom with you. Those that walk with you will speak. Those that stand by the path to give direction will speak. I embrace you and I wrap my blanket around you. The blanket of love. Feel its warmth and when you are afraid, draw it close.

Hear me. For I have spoken.

Ho!

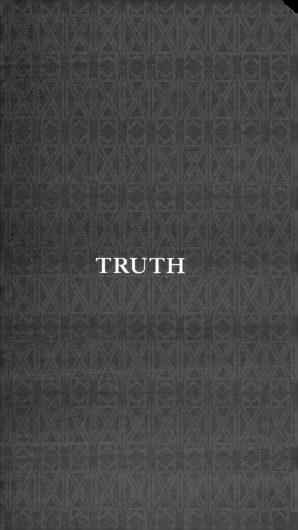

TRUTH

Hear me my son,
hear me my daughter.
You reach into the nothingness
of the past and you step
into the nothingness of the
future. For in your thoughts
now is what is yet to be.

Love oneself in totality,
embrace the strengths and
weaknesses of self.
For to love oneself is to
love the Great Spirit from
which all life comes.

For know this.
What emanates from
you returns to you.
If it is love, love must return.
If it is anger, anger will return.
For that is the power
of your thoughts.

Send out your love.
For the love that is given without
thought, the love that asks nothing
in return, is the purest love.
It is the love that nourishes
the souls of the unborn, that
attracts them to enter the
wombs of the mothers.

My children.
Our Mother Earth
breathes as do you.
Our Mother Earth feels as do you.
For without nourishment,
all life withers.
Each one of you contributes.
Do not think what you
contribute is nothing.
For a great avalanche starts
with but a small stone.
As you can heal one another, so
can you heal our Mother Earth.

Humankind are born in
innocence and born in totality.
Yet they spend their lives
as beggars, for they cannot
recognise the beauty of self.

Take this power of creation.
Take this gift that was
given you and truly you
will walk in paradise.
And your children's children will
walk in peace for a thousand years.

Many of you have seen tears
and disappointments.
You regret that which was.
You gaze upon your mistakes
and you carry your guilt.
But were they mistakes?
Or did you make them
that you might learn?

Your logicality allows you only to
see that which your eyes perceive
and that which your ears can hear.
But if you walk with us
you will see all life.
For the speck of dust that
dances within the sunbeam
is a world unto itself.
There are, my children, worlds
within worlds and worlds again.

If you listen you will hear the
silent voice of Divinity itself.
That you are eternal.
That you are upon
the wheel of life.
That you were never born
and can never die.

Know this my children.
The Great Spirit is not
separate from you.
For you shine with his brilliance
and you breathe with his breath
and you speak with his voice.

Do not think that what you have
to contribute is insignificant.
For without you there can
be no completion.
As the stars in heaven are in
their appointed places, so you
are in your appointed place.

The purpose of life is to live.
To live in freedom, to become
that which you are.

Stand straight and tall.
Not the reflection as others see
you, but as you truly are.

You are part of the Great Spirit.
He does not know how to punish.
It is you that sits in
judgement of you.
It is you that punishes you.

Love yourselves, but not
the love of arrogance.
The love of recognising
the beauty that you are.

All that exists in this infinitesimal second is you. What lays before you is life.

Nothing is separate.
You are the light and you
are the darkness.
You are the joy and you
are the sorrow.
Nothing is in isolation.

There is only this moment and in this moment you create.

And so you created circumstances.
Those who have brought you
sadness, disappointment and tears
were of equal worth with those
who brought you love and success.

It takes a warrior to walk this path.
For a warrior has been
tested many times.
He has journeyed inside himself
and sought out his strengths and
weaknesses as you have done.

You have known sadness
and disappointment,
disillusionment and anger.
But you have found the courage
to pass through the pain and
stand tall and straight.

The time for words has passed.
Now you must walk your
words and live your truth.

Now you have begun
to remember.
Now our mother calls and you
draw closer and thus your heart
attunes itself to the voice of life.

For I speak with the voice
of the Great Spirit and I
speak with the voice of the
mountains and the rivers.
For I speak with the voice
of all life, as you speak with
the voice of all life.
Recognise your power.

You are the Great Spirit.
Create your beauty.
You are perfection.
Recognise this.

You are free, my children,
to fly with the eagles, to
soar with the hawks.
And the time will come when the
great forests will return, and the
animals will come once again and
share their wisdom with you.
Nothing is separate.
Hear me my children.
Grandfather eagle flies above you!

LOVE YOURSELF

Be cautious with your
thoughts for they can destroy
and bring great pain.
These same thoughts can heal
and create many wonders.
Indeed, all is choice.

You are free.
Only the illusion of restraint
holds you in darkness.

How can one be loved
until one knows love?
And how can one know love
until one loves oneself?

Remember my words.
Know that you are precious to me.
Know that I share my
blanket with you.

This is my energy, and
this is my strength.
The strength of the mountains
and the oceans and the forests.
The strength of the unborn.
Draw it into your beings.
Rise up with us.
For we are many and we are love.
If you are afraid to live, then
life will pass from you.

When you make decisions in
your life, go to a quiet place.
Bring your heart and
mind together.
Cast aside the logicality of
thought for it is the logical mind
that has imprisoned man.

You were created in the
image of the Great Spirit.
You are divine.
Allow the divinity that
resides within all men and
women to emerge.
There is nothing you
cannot accomplish.
Allow the universe to flow
through you my children.
For it is the river of life.
The gifts of the universe
are infinite.

The time has come for you to
accept responsibility for your life.
And in doing so, become free.
For you are free, my children, as
free as the hawk and the eagle.

When you love yourself,
others will love you.
Others will respect you.
And when you choose, you not
only enhance your own life, you
send out energies that others, in a
sad place in their lives, can reach
out for and bring into their reality.

The choices you make are a
reflection of how you see yourself.
Of how you believe others see you.
Can you not see that if you look
inside self and accept self and
learn to love and respect self,
then your choices become easy.

Know that there is
only one energy.
If you see yourself as unworthy,
that is the reality that you will live.

The same energy that
creates, destroys.
The energy that brings
sadness and sickness can
bring health and happiness.
There is not good.
There is not evil.
There is energy.
Use it as you wish.

I have spoken that we do not
impose ourselves upon you, and
you should not impose yourself
upon another or allow another to
impose themselves upon you.

You were created in the
image of the Great Spirit.
You are perfection.
You are limitless.

Each second is a new beginning.
Rid yourself, therefore,
of the past.
Become what you truly are.

There is nothing preordained.
The life that was given to you
is a gift to use as you wish.
It is you that creates the future.
What lays before you is nothing.
And you create your future
from this nothingness, for in
truth, that is all there is.

Shrug off the restraints that
you have allowed others
to place upon you.
You are limitless.
There is nothing you
cannot achieve.
There is no sadness in life
that cannot be reversed.
There is no sickness that
cannot be cured.
Each second you can be reborn.
Each second there can
be a new beginning.
It is choice.
It is your choice.

Above all, be patient
with yourself.
Gaze back upon the path
that brought you to this
place and this time.
Gaze then into the night sky.
See the stars in all their glory.
Marvel at them as they are
part of the universe, placed
there by the Great Spirit.
Then, my children, gaze upon
yourself, at the wondrous
creation that you are.
You are part of this universe.
Without you the universe
is not complete.

Escape from the dungeon
of your mind.
Reach into your heart, for
within you is the memory
of many lifetimes.
There is nothing separate.
All is connected.

For the bond of love is eternal
and cannot be severed.
If you reach out with your heart
to the universe, you can return to
your rightful place in the universe.

Give thanks to the universe
for what you are.
Know that you have
your part to play.
Know that you are divine.
Know that what you are is eternal.
That you travel on through space,
that you have much to contribute.

In coming to recognise the self,
the wonder of self, then that
which you choose becomes easy.

Why are you afraid?
The life that was given to you
by the Great Spirit was a gift
to do with as you wish.
Your thought is your magic.
Your thought is energy.
Create your paradise.

The past, the present and
the future are one.
Live in the moment, my children.
Use the gift of creation
to create paradise.

Know that humankind is
but one manifestation of
the force of life itself.
Know that all life is connected.

Children, hear me.
The secret of life is love.
It is so simple.
Is is so simple that it is
difficult to comprehend.

What is fear?
A shadow.
It has no substance.
To give it substance draws upon
you what you fear the most.

START TO LIVE

Man speaks of miracles,
but is he not a miracle?

You are part of the Great Spirit.
You are perfection, yet you
have allowed others to place
limitations upon you.
Now is the time of awareness.
Now is the time for remembrance.
You have chosen this.
No other can choose it for you.

Trust yourself.
Trust your own knowing.
Take it by the hand and follow it.
Listen and you will hear
the silent voice that speaks
to you from your heart.
Follow it and you will
know great beauty.

Do not live in the
shadow of the past.
Learn from it.
Bless it.
Thank it for the lessons
it has taught you.
Thank it for your sadnesses,
for your failures, for your joys
and for your successes.

Learn from the past.
Learn from the sadnesses, the
disappointments, the tears,
the successes, the joys.
And release them all.
Do not carry them in your
mind and in your heart.
Instead see anew.
Feel anew.
Create wonders.

Learn to love and respect yourself.
In this way you will come to
understand that what you do to
yourself you do unto another.

Speak to the Great Spirit.
Speak words of love
and of gratitude.
Place not one morsel upon your
tongue nor one stick upon your
fires without giving thanks.
For they are the gifts, my children.

My children, you live your
life in a reality of illusions.
You and you alone create
and manifest your fears.
There is no death, there is
no sickness, save that which
is created by man's logical,
conscious thought.

Accept your lives.
Take them back from those
that would manipulate you.
No one sees through your eyes.
No one knows what you
carry in your heart.
You are unique.
Yet in this uniqueness you
are the same as all others.
You are part of the whole.

Live in the moment
and in the now.
Create what is to be.
For nothing is preordained.
It is you that chooses
what is to come.

All is choice.
But care must be taken
in the choosing.
In the choosing you cannot
choose for another.

Man yearns to return
to the self within.
And on this journey he will find
that all there is dwells within him.

You were given the greatest
gift of all my children.
The gift of creation.
Use the magic that is your gift.
Send it out to those that
suffer pain and sickness.
Know that you can raise them
above death itself, for sickness and
death are the creation of mankind.

If you believe you must know
pain before you can know joy,
pain is what you will create.
Such is your power.
If you believe you can walk
in love and beauty and
harmony, it will be so.
Such is your power.
If you believe you must walk
in loneliness and in poverty, it
will be so. Such is your power.

Even in your weakness there
is great beauty within you.
For in that beauty
there is strength.
Strength to create many wonders
that open many doors for your
children's children to walk in
paradise, to walk with other
intelligences and walk in love.

Yesterday is the husks that
held the seeds of today.
Take the seeds.
Nurture them.
Let the husks blow away.

Create joys.
Start to live.
From this day forward walk
as one with all things.
Reach out and touch with
your thoughts, with your
mind, with your heart.

Take the gifts of the
universe, my children.
Use them.
Become the example.

There is nothing I can tell you
that you do not already know.
There is no question that
you can ask me that you
yourself cannot answer.
You have just forgotten.

You have forgotten to allow the river of life to flow through you, to open your hearts to the seasons, to know that you are on the wheel of life that has no beginning and that has no end. Know that the time of parting comes at the time of choosing. Know too, that you are eternal.

You are not alone.
Not for one second in all eternity.
And in your darkest time you
are the least alone of all.
But he that walks beside you
reaches out, yet he cannot touch
you until you reach out.

Know that you are part
of the universe.
Know that other dimensions
reach out to you.
The beings of light
walk among you.
The creatures of the stars, the
creatures of the oceans, they
reach out to touch your heart.
They touch you with love
and compassion to show
you all life is sacred.

Life is like a ripe fruit that
hangs upon the bough.
Reach out and it will fall
into your hands.
Hesitate and it will wither.

The severity of lessons
is your choice.

Learn from the past.
Do not come to the end of your
life only to find you have not lived.
For many come to the point of
leaving the space of the earth
and when they gaze back, they
see the joy and the beauty that
could not be theirs because
of the fears they lived.

Man sees an end and
sees a beginning.
It is not so.
You are upon the wheel of life.
The beginning is the end.
The end is the beginning.

Only by finding the source of life within yourself do you once again become part of the universe.

TAKE MY HAND

Do not speak in a loud voice.
Let your thoughts be quiet,
then those that have need
of you will find you.

Go quietly about your
lives knowing that you are
worthy and in so doing,
empower those around you
to seek their own worth.

In me you see yourselves, then
my voice becomes your voice.
For I reflect the love that you seek.

Reach out with your thoughts and in so doing bring aid to the sick and comfort to the dying.

Remember my children, I
come from the grandfathers
to show you once again the
ways of the people that walked
in harmony with all life.

Nothing is separate.
All life comes from the
one creation itself.
No one life form holds
domain over another.
Each one has its part to play.

All life forms have a voice.
If you are quiet they will share
their wisdom with you.

A lie can slip as easy from the
tongue as can the truth.
Gaze into another's eyes
to see the truth.

You are eternal.
Only your shape and
form ever changes.

You that have walked on four legs and flown on feathered wings, now walk the path of remembrance. Do so in gentleness for you cannot imagine what you are yet to be.

You will never fulfil the
expectations of self.

You are but one emanation
of the countless life forms
in the universe.

My children, how will you
know life until you have
seen through every eye.

To condemn and judge another is to condemn and judge oneself.

Would you punish a child
for falling as it takes its
first hesitant step?
Then why do you punish
yourselves so harshly when
you stumble and fall?

It was you that chose the seed
from which you would spring
and the womb that would
give you shape and form.

Life is for living.
It can not be described, for it is a
thing of feelings and sensations.

You are at this very moment,
all that you have ever been and
all that you are yet to be.

For, is not the man within the boy, awaiting his moment to emerge?

Is not the flower within the bud?
Yet if you were to tear
apart the bud the flower
would not be found.

Your eyes only perceive the surface of each moment, look into its depth to see its true meaning.

Your reality is created by
your thoughts, yet love comes
unbidden, for its source is
the place of feelings.

It is foolishness to wear the mask of deceit and try to be as another would have you be, for you are you, and what you are yet to be.

Let those that follow in your footsteps honour your memory. Walk with honour and respect upon the earth, for it is the home of those yet unborn.

The time will pass when men benefit from the misfortune of others.

The pain that man inflicts upon
any life form will return in kind.
For all things return
to their source.

Now is the moment to
reach beyond the accepted,
beyond the known and
explore the unimagined.

Rid yourself of expectations
for they are formed by
past experiences.
You cannot enter the new
when burdened by the past.

Who amongst you has the courage to take my hand and enter into what lays beyond? I come to guide you out of the valley of shadows, up to the high places above the clouds where you can see eternity.

Remember my children.
I have no power over you.
If you chose to take my hand
then do so willingly for I
ask only for your trust.
Allow the river of life to flow.
Let it carry you to the
place of your dreams.

For further information,
channellings and to hear
Clearwater speak please visit:
wordsofclearwater.com

or Instagram:
wordsofclearwater

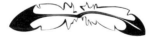